S0-AWP-895

BUMPER ALL IN ONE

This book belongs to

Name _____

Class _____ Sec. _____

School _____

_____

tricolor BOOKS

CONTENTS

A a

Apple

B b

Ball

C c

Cat

D d

Dog

tricolor

ALL IN ONE

E e

Elephant

F f

Fa

G g

Grapes

H h

Hen

ALL IN ONE

tricolor

I i

Ice-cream

J j

Jug

K k

Kite

L l

Lion

Mm

Mango

Nn

Nest

Oo

Orange

Pp

Parrot

Q q

Queen

R r

Rabbit

S s

Ship

T t

Tiger

ALL IN ONE

U u

Umbrella

V v

Van

W w

Watch

X x

X-mas tree

Y y

Yak

Z z

Zebra

ALL IN ONE

tricolor

अ  अनार	आ  आम
इ  इमली	ई  ईख
उ  उल्लू	ऊ ऊन

ALL IN ONE

tricolor

छ

छतरी

ज

जहाज

झ

झंडा

ट

टमाटर

ठ

ठठेरा

ड

डमरू

ढ

ढक्कन

ढ़

ण

त

तरबूज

थ

थरमस

द

दवात

ध

धनुष

ALL IN ONE

tricolor

न  नल	प  पतंग
फ  फल	ब  बत्तख
भ भगत	म  मछली

ALL IN ONE

tricolor

य

यज्ञ

र

रथ

ल

लट्टू

व

वक

श

शलगम

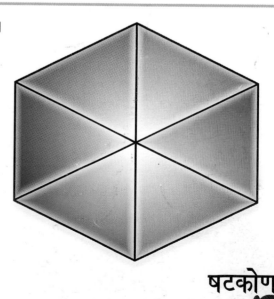

ष

षटकोण

tricolor

ALL IN ONE

स

सपेरा

ह

हल

क्ष

क्षत्रिय

त्र

त्रिशूल

ज्ञ

ज्ञानी

श्र

श्रमिक

ALL IN ONE

tricolor

1

ONE

2

TWO

3

THREE

4

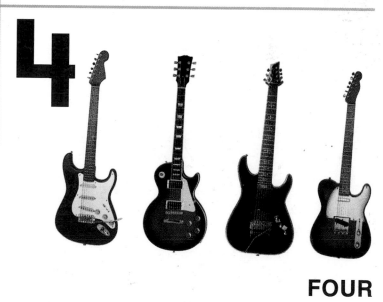

FOUR

5

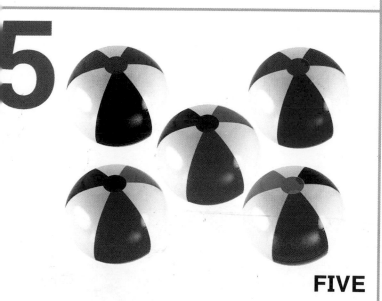

FIVE

6

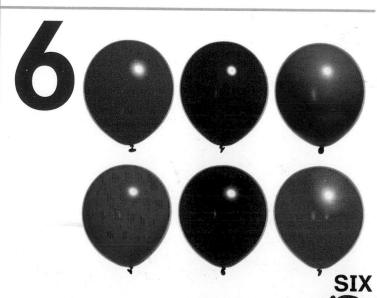

SIX

ALL IN ONE

7

SEVEN

8

EIGHT

9

NINE

10

TEN

11
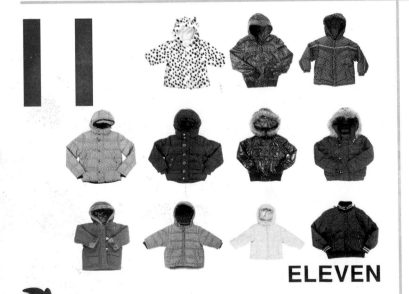
ELEVEN

12

TWELVE

ALL IN ONE

tricolor

13
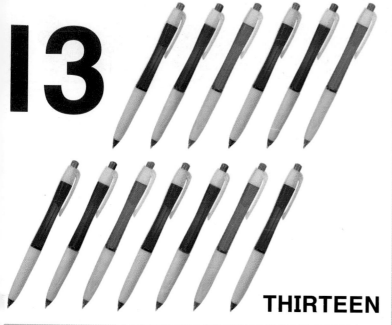
THIRTEEN

14

FOURTEEN

15

FIFTEEN

16
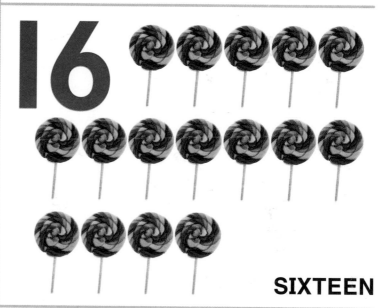
SIXTEEN

17

SEVENTEEN

18

EIGHTEEN

tricolor

ALL IN ONE

19 NINETEEN

20 TWENTY

ALL IN ONE

tricolor

MULTIPLICATION TABLES

TABLE OF 1

1 X 1 = 1	1 One is 1
1 X 2 = 2	1 Two is 2
1 X 3 = 3	1 Three is 3
1 X 4 = 4	1 Four is 4
1 X 5 = 5	1 Five is 5
1 X 6 = 6	1 Six is 6
1 X 7 = 7	1 Seven is 7
1 X 8 = 8	1 Eight is 8
1 X 9 = 9	1 Nine is 9
1 X10 =10	1 Ten is 10

TABLE OF 2

2 X 1 = 2	2 Ones are 2
2 X 2 = 4	2 Twos are 4
2 X 3 = 6	2 Threes are 6
2 X 4 = 8	2 Fours are 8
2 X 5 = 10	2 Fives are 10
2 X 6 = 12	2 Sixes are 12
2 X 7 = 14	2 Sevens are 14
2 X 8 = 16	2 Eights are 16
2 X 9 = 18	2 Nines are 18
2 X10 = 20	2 Tens are 20

ALL IN ONE

trícolor

3 TABLE OF 3

3 X 1 = 3	3 Ones are 3
3 X 2 = 6	3 Twos are 6
3 X 3 = 9	3 Threes are 9
3 X 4 = 12	3 Fours are 12
3 X 5 = 15	3 Fives are 15
3 X 6 = 18	3 Sixes are 18
3 X 7 = 21	3 Sevens are 21
3 X 8 = 24	3 Eights are 24
3 X 9 = 27	3 Nines are 27
3 X10 = 30	3 Tens are 30

4 TABLE OF 4

4 X 1 = 4	4 Ones are 4
4 X 2 = 8	4 Twos are 8
4 X 3 = 12	4 Threes are 12
4 X 4 = 16	4 Fours are 16
4 X 5 = 20	4 Fives are 20
4 X 6 = 24	4 Sixes are 24
4 X 7 = 28	4 Sevens are 28
4 X 8 = 32	4 Eights are 32
4 X 9 = 36	4 Nines are 36
4 X10 = 40	4 Tens are 40

tricolor

5 TABLE OF 5

5 X	1	=	5	5 Ones are	5
5 X	2	=	10	5 Twos are	10
5 X	3	=	15	5 Threes are	15
5 X	4	=	20	5 Fours are	20
5 X	5	=	25	5 Fives are	25
5 X	6	=	30	5 Sixes are	30
5 X	7	=	35	5 Sevens are	35
5 X	8	=	40	5 Eights are	40
5 X	9	=	45	5 Nines are	45
5 X	10	=	50	5 Tens are	50

6 TABLE OF 6

6 X	1	=	6	6 Ones are	6
6 X	2	=	12	6 Twos are	12
6 X	3	=	18	6 Threes are	18
6 X	4	=	24	6 Fours are	24
6 X	5	=	30	6 Fives are	30
6 X	6	=	36	6 Sixes are	36
6 X	7	=	42	6 Sevens are	42
6 X	8	=	48	6 Eights are	48
6 X	9	=	54	6 Nines are	54
6 X	10	=	60	6 Tens are	60

tricolor

ALL IN ONE

TABLE OF 7

7 X	1	=	7	7 Ones are	7
7 X	2	=	14	7 Twos are	14
7 X	3	=	21	7 Threes are	21
7 X	4	=	28	7 Fours are	28
7 X	5	=	35	7 Fives are	35
7 X	6	=	42	7 Sixes are	42
7 X	7	=	49	7 Sevens are	49
7 X	8	=	56	7 Eights are	56
7 X	9	=	63	7 Nines are	63
7 X	10	=	70	7 Tens are	70

TABLE OF 8

8 X	1	=	8	8 Ones are	8
8 X	2	=	16	8 Twos are	16
8 X	3	=	24	8 Threes are	24
8 X	4	=	32	8 Fours are	32
8 X	5	=	40	8 Fives are	40
8 X	6	=	48	8 Sixes are	48
8 X	7	=	56	8 Sevens are	56
8 X	8	=	64	8 Eights are	64
8 X	9	=	72	8 Nines are	72
8 X	10	=	80	8 Tens are	80

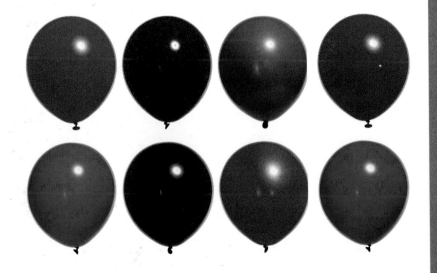

trikolor

TABLE OF 9

9 X 1 = 9	9 Ones are 9
9 X 2 = 18	9 Twos are 18
9 X 3 = 27	9 Threes are 27
9 X 4 = 36	9 Fours are 36
9 X 5 = 45	9 Fives are 45
9 X 6 = 54	9 Sixes are 54
9 X 7 = 63	9 Sevens are 63
9 X 8 = 72	9 Eights are 72
9 X 9 = 81	9 Nines are 81
9 X 10 = 90	9 Tens are 90

TABLE OF 10

10 X 1 = 10	10 Ones are 10
10 X 2 = 20	10 Twos are 20
10 X 3 = 30	10 Threes are 30
10 X 4 = 40	10 Fours are 40
10 X 5 = 50	10 Fives are 50
10 X 6 = 60	10 Sixes are 60
10 X 7 = 70	10 Sevens are 70
10 X 8 = 80	10 Eights are 80
10 X 9 = 90	10 Nines are 90
10 X 10 = 100	10 Tens are 100

COLOURS

RED

YELLOW

BLUE

GREEN

PURPLE

ORANGE

BROWN

PINK

BLACK

WHITE

GOLDEN

SILVER

ALL IN ONE

tricolor

SHAPES

CIRCLE

SEMI-CIRCLE

SQUARE

TRIANGLE

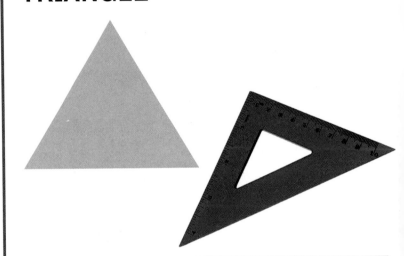

RECTANGLE

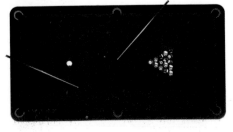

OVAL

ALL IN ONE

tricolor

CUBE

CUBOID

SPHERE

HEMISPHERE

CYLINDER

FRESH LEMON

CONE

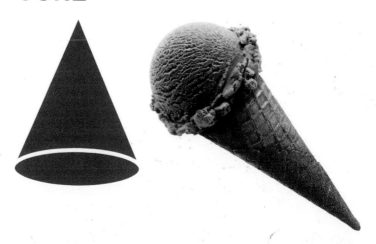

tricolor

ALL IN ONE

BODY PARTS

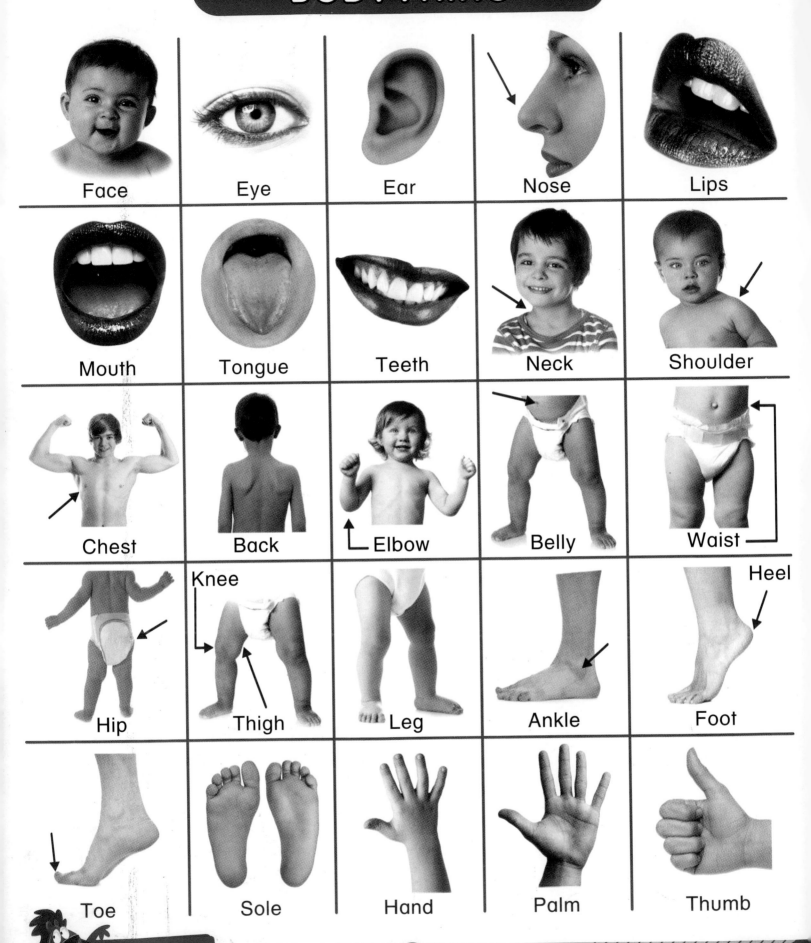

Face	Eye	Ear	Nose	Lips
Mouth	Tongue	Teeth	Neck	Shoulder
Chest	Back	Elbow	Belly	Waist
Hip	Knee Thigh	Leg	Ankle	Heel Foot
Toe	Sole	Hand	Palm	Thumb

ALL IN ONE

tricolor

MY FAMILY

Grandfather   Grandmother   Father   Mother

Uncle

Aunt

Brother   Sister

Cousin

ALL IN ONE

tricolor

CLOTHES WE WEAR

Shirt

Jeans

Sweater

Gloves

Lehenga

Saree

T-shirt

Frock

Jacket

Nightsuit

Bib

Coat

Socks

Shoes

Romper

ALL IN ONE

tricolor

VEGETARIAN FOOD

Rice

Subji

Milk

Sandwich

Ice-cream

Cheese

Chapati

Butter

Honey

Bread

Soup

Pudding

Pudding

Noodles

Juice

Popcorn

Pickle

Pasta

Salad

Pizza

tricolor

ALL IN ONE

NON-VEGETARIAN FOOD

Butter Chicken

Boiled Egg

Prawn

Seekh Kebab

Chicken Biryani

Chicken Masala

Chicken Drumstick

Egg Curry

Fish Curry

Fish Fry

Mutton Curry

Mutton

Omelette

CEREALS, PULSES & SPICES

Cereal Grains

| Barley | Oat | Wheat | Rice | Maize |

Pulses

| Chick Peas | Red Kidney Beans | Black Eyed Beans |

| Red Lentil | Moong Beans | Split Yellow Peas | Black Lentil |

Spices

| Chilli Powder | Salt | Turmeric |

| Black Pepper | Big Cardamom | Cloves | Star Anise |

ALL IN ONE

FRUITS

Orange

Watermelon

Apple

Banana

Chikoo

Mango

Guava

Cherry

Pomegranate

Grapes

Papaya

ALL IN ONE

Tricolor

Physalis

Pear

Strawberry

Lychee

Star Fruit

Peach

Plum

Raspberry

Kiwi

Custard Apple

Loquat

Pineapple

tricolor books

ALL IN ONE

VEGETABLES

Tomato

Carrots

Peas

Spinach

Beetroot

Pumpkin

Brinjal

Lady Finger

Cucumber

Potato

Onion

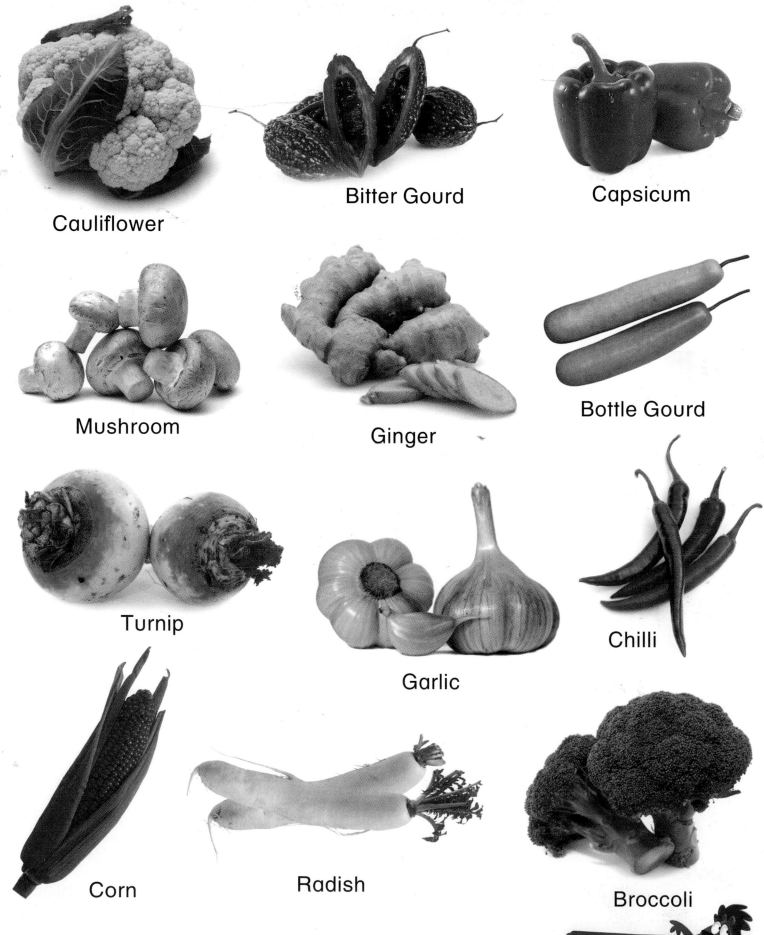

Cauliflower

Bitter Gourd

Capsicum

Mushroom

Ginger

Bottle Gourd

Turnip

Garlic

Chilli

Corn

Radish

Broccoli

tricolor

ALL IN ONE

NUTS & DRYFRUITS

Walnuts

Pistachio Nuts

Pecan Nuts

Cashew Nuts

Almonds

Peanuts

Dates

Raisins

Dried Apricot

Betel Nuts

Pine nut

Coconut

tricolor

MY TOYS

Building Blocks

Tricycle

Doll

Ball

Car

Scooty

Abacus

Aeroplane

Train

Swing

Yo-Yo

Top

Xylophone

Teddy Bear

ALL IN ONE

tricolor

Wall

Roof

Floor

Door

Window

Stairs

Bedroom

Kitchen

Bathroom

Toilet

Drawing Room

Dining Room

FISH

Tuna

Trout

Pomfret

Sardine

Barracuda

Pufferfish

Piranha

Pike

Halibut

Carp

Goldfish

Codfish

Shark

Clownfish

Bass

Catfish

Starfish

Marlin

Flounder

Dolphin

tricolor

ALL IN ONE

WILD ANIMALS

Lion

Deer

Zebra

Hippopotamus

Monkey

Tiger

Kangaroo

Bear

Elephant

Giraffe

tricolor

Wolf

Porcupine

Reindeer

Boar

Panda

Fox

Gorilla

Rhinoceros

tricolor

ALL IN ONE

DOMESTIC ANIMALS

Dog

Camel

Cat

Buffalo

Sheep

Horse

Donkey

Goat

Cow

ALL IN ONE

46

tricolor

Pig

Rabbit

Guinea Pig

Ferret

Mink

Fancy Rat

Bison

Llama

Yak

tricolor books

ALL IN ONE

ANIMALS & THEIR YOUNG ONES

Lion-Cub

Dog-Puppy

Horse-Foal

Cow-Calf

Donkey-Foal

Rhinoceros-Calf

Goat-Kid

Rabbit-Kit

Sheep-Lamb

Zebra-Foal

Cat-Kitten

Hen-Chicken

tricolor books

Monkey-Infant

Pig-Piglet

Kangaroo-Joey

Elephant- Calf

Giraffe-Giraffeling

Tiger-Cub

Panda-Cub

Polar Bear-Cub

Peafowl-Peachick

Owl-Owlet

Butterfly-Caterpillar

Yak-Calf

ALL IN ONE

Horse (Stable)

Honey Bee (Beehive)

Hen (Coop)

Duck (Pond)

Dog (Kennel)

Cat (Cattery)

Bird (Nest)

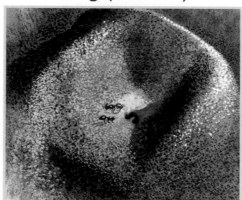
Ant (Formicary)

Bear (Den)

Donkey (Paddock)

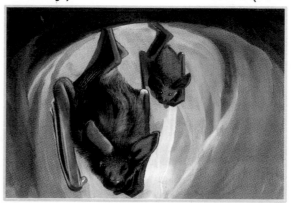
Bat (Roost)

ALL IN ONE

SOUNDS OF ANIMALS

Roars — Lion

Hoots — Owl

Whoops — Monkey

Bleats — Goat

Squawks — Parrot

Neighs — Horse

Moos — Cow

Trumpets — Elephant

Sparrow

Crow

Hen

Frog

House Fly

Snake

Cat

Dog

Donkey

BIRDS

Peacock

Swan

Hen

Pigeon

Sparrow

Lorikeet

Duck

Crow

Blue Jay

Budgerigar

Parrot

Hoopoe

Owl

Weaver Bird

Turkey

Eagle

Penguin

ALL IN ONE

Macaw

Toucan

Kingfisher

Heron

Woodpecker

Flamingo

Ostrich

Canary

Robin

Vulture

Pelican

Nightingale

Mynah

Hawk

tricolor

ALL IN ONE

FLOWERS

Dahlia

Daisy

Rose

Lotus

Lily

Sunflower

Orchid

Tulip

Bougainvillea

ALL IN ONE

Gladiolus

Zinnia

Daffodil

Flamingo

Blue Water Lily

Chrysanthemum

Lavender

Aster

Poppy

ALL IN ONE

SEA ANIMALS

Dolphin

Octopus

Sea Horse

Snail

Fish

Crab

Toad

Turtle

Star Fish

Shark

ALL IN ONE

Walrus

Shellfish

Lobster

Sea Snake

Seal (Sea lion)

Jellyfish

Coral

Whale

Marlin

Squid

ALL IN ONE

INSECTS

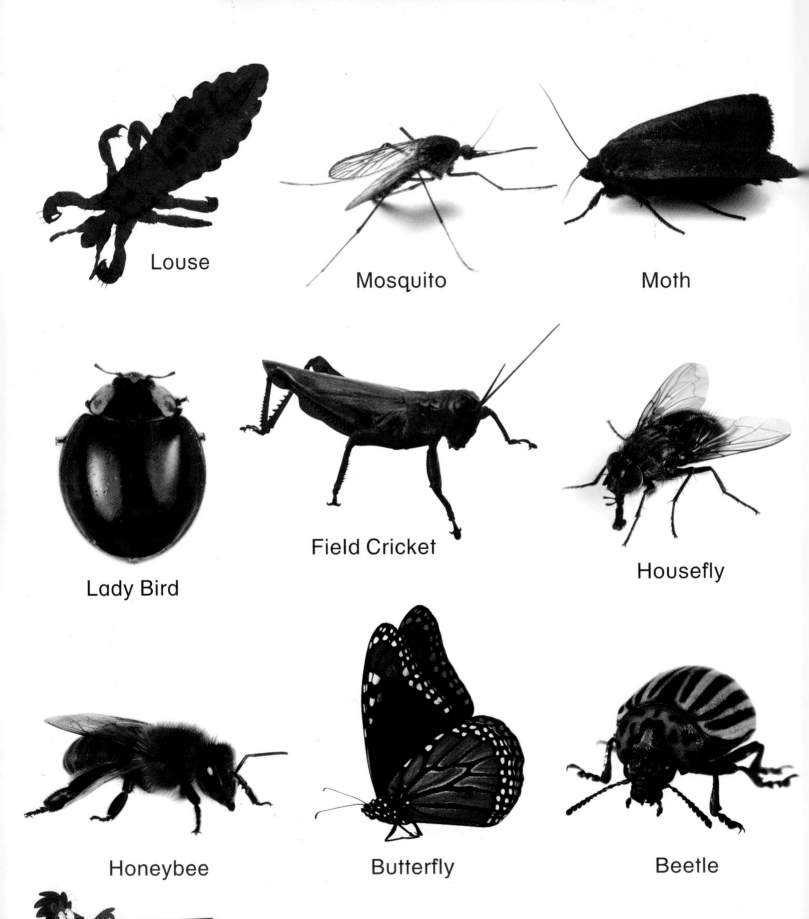

Louse

Mosquito

Moth

Lady Bird

Field Cricket

Housefly

Honeybee

Butterfly

Beetle

tricolor

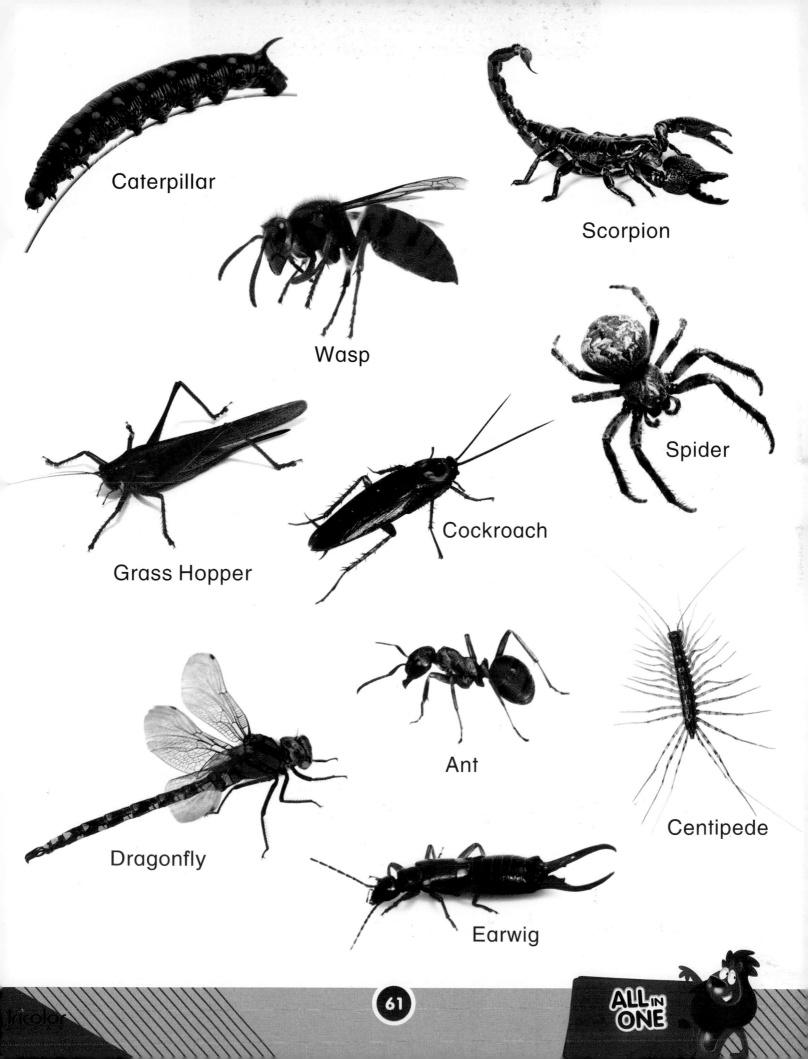

Caterpillar

Scorpion

Wasp

Spider

Grass Hopper

Cockroach

Dragonfly

Ant

Centipede

Earwig

ALL IN ONE

tricolor

Chameleon

Snake

Tortoise

Gavial

Lizard

Newt

Gecko

Salamander

Caecilian

Frilled lizard

Iguana

Toad

Gila Monster

Alligator

Crocodile

Frog

ALL IN ONE

VEHICLES

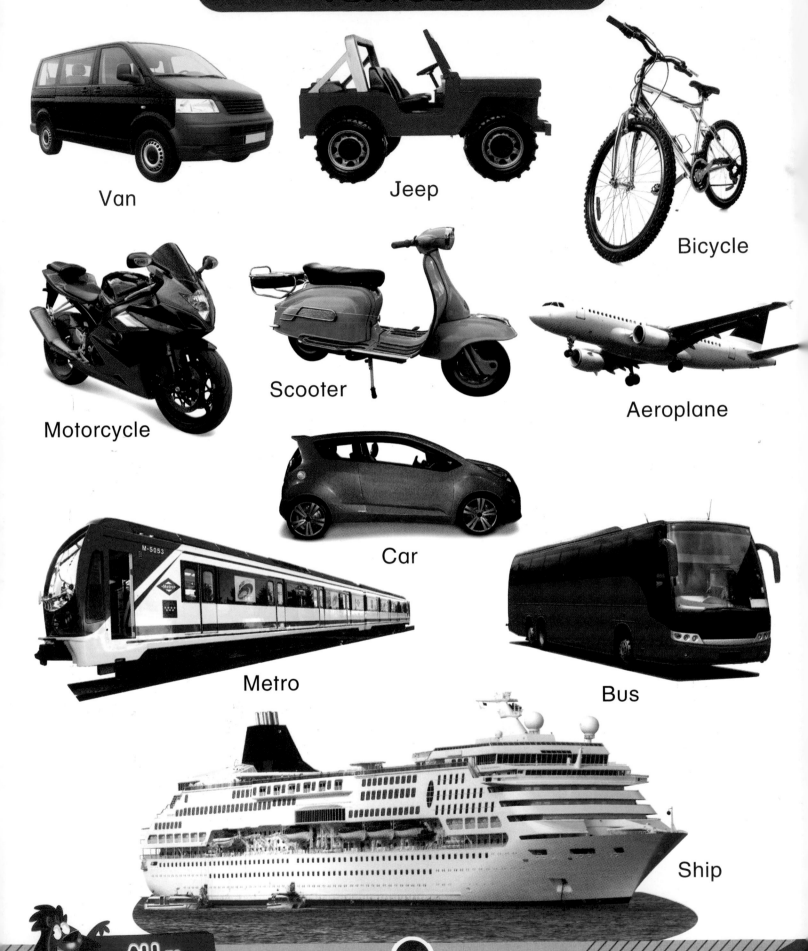

Van

Jeep

Bicycle

Motorcycle

Scooter

Aeroplane

Car

Metro

Bus

Ship

ACTION WORDS

| Drinking | Eating | Clapping | Bending |

| Walking | Running | Jumping | Laughing |

| Crying | Throwing | Catching | Acting |

ALL IN ONE

Pulling   Exercising   Jogging   Dancing

Writing   Standing   Somersaulting   Climbing

Skipping   Sliding   Skating   Reading

ALL IN ONE

Blowing

Rocking

Kicking

Scratching

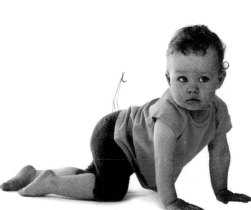

Crawling

Playing

Kneeling

Sitting

Juggling

Singing

ALL IN ONE

tricolor

OPPOSITES

Boy   Girl   Strong   Weak   Sit   Stand

Up   Down   Cry   Laugh   Wet   Dry

Give   Take   Hot   Cold   Small   Big

Left   Right

Open

Close

Full

Empty

Fat   Thin

Short   Tall

Happy

Sad

Sweet

Dirty

Young

Bitter

Clean

Old

ALL IN ONE

tricolor

Throw

Catch

Bend

Straight

Push

Pull

Many

Soft

Slow

Few

Hard

Fast

In

Black

Front

Back

Out

White

GOOD HABITS

Get up early in the morning.

Brush your teeth every morning and every night before going to bed.

Take bath everyday.

Put on clean clothes and polished shoes.

Exercise everyday.

Do your work yourself.

tricolor

ALL IN ONE

Always maintain right posture.

Keep your things in place.

Save your pocket money.

Play outdoor games.

Comb your hair nicely.

Pray to God.

Eat healthy foods like green
vegetables, salads, milk, etc.

Drink plenty of water.

Go to school on time.

Have your meals on time.

Throw trash in the bin.

Trim your nails regularly.

Wash your hands
before and after meals.

Do your work neatly and regularly.

Read before you go to bed.

Always sleep on time.

ALL IN ONE

GOOD MANNERS

Greet your elders.

Always greet your teachers.

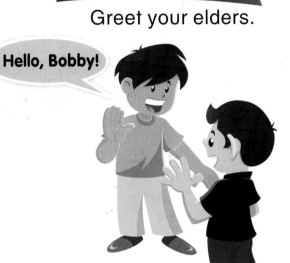

Greet your friends nicely.

Always help your friends.

Help elders.

Say 'Excuse me' if you want someone to move out of your path.

Offer your seat to the elders.

Allow elders to let in while you open the door for them.

Ask for permission before you borrow something.

Always return things that you've borrowed.

Don't bully animals, treat them well.

Apologise for your mistakes.

ALL IN ONE

Always share.

Wait for your turn while talking.

Ask for permission before you enter.

Do not jump the queue.

Show sportsman spirit.

Use handkerchief while coughing or sneezing.

ANIMALS & THEIR HOUSES

Tiger (Lair)

Squirrel (Drey)

Spider (Web)

Sheep (Pen)

Rat (Hole)

Rabbit (Burrow)

Pig (Sty)

Otter (Holt)

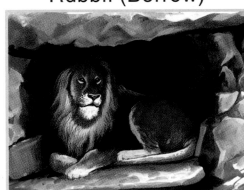
Lion (Den)

Goat (Barn)

Cow (Cowshed)

SAFETY MEASURES

Remember your address, telephone number and your parents' full names.

POLICE = 100
AMBULANCE = 101
FIRE BRIGADE = 102
C... = 1099

Know all the emergency numbers.

Don't use the cell phone while charging. It may explode.

Use scissors carefully. Never use blade for cutting. It can wound your fingers.

Never play with plastic bags. They can choke you.

Watch out for toys that have sharp edges, small parts or sharp points. They can hurt.

tricolor

ALL IN ONE

Don't fly kites from the terrace walls. You can fall.

Do not play on the roads. Moving vehicles could be dangerous.

Keep away from open or loose electric wires. You can get a shock.

Watch TV from a safe distance. It will not harm your eyes.

Don't talk to strangers.

Never leave your parents in crowded places. You can get lost.

Never play in deserted
buildings or isolated areas.

Always fasten your seat
belts, when in a car.

Never touch anything that doesn't
belong to you. It could be dangerous.

Don't tease animals,
they may harm you.

Always cross a road at the zebra
crossing. Never run on the road.

Light fireworks always
under adult supervision.

SEASONS

Summer

Winter

Spring

Autumn

Rainy

tricolor

FESTIVALS

Holi

Diwali

Eid

Ramnavami

Christmas

Dussehra

Onam

Independence Day

Pongal

Lohri

Mahavir Jayanti

Raksha Bandhan

OUR HELPERS

Doctor

Teacher

Soldier

Pilot

Milkman

Firefighter

Postman

Electrician

Plumber

Mason

Photographer

Gardener

Chef

Tailor

Painter

Traffic Guard

SOURCES OF WATER

Lake

Pond

Sea

Rain

River

Well

Water Tap

Hand Pump

PLACES OF WORSHIP

Temple

Gurudwara

Mosque

Church

Bahai Temple

Jain Temple

Synagogue

Vihara

ALL IN ONE

tricolor

COMPUTER PARTS & PERIPHERALS

Monitor

CPU

UPS

DVD

Laptop

Scanner

Pen Drive

Printer

Speakers

Modem

Keyboard

Mouse

Motherboard

ALL IN ONE

tricolor

HISTORICAL PLACES

Taj Mahal (Agra)

Qutub Minar (New Delhi)

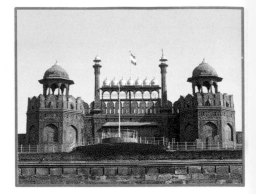
Red Fort (New Delhi)

Old Fort (New Delhi)

Charminar (Hyderabad)

Gateway of India (Mumbai)

Hawa Mahal (Jaipur)

Victoria Memorial (Kolkata)

Howrah Bridge (Kolkata)

Sanchi Stupa (Sanchi)

Meenakshi Temple (Madurai)

Sun Temple (Konark)

NATIONAL SYMBOLS OF INDIA

National Flag (Tricolour)

National Emblem (Ashoka Chinha)

National Flower (Lotus)

National Animal (Tiger)

National Bird (Peacock)

National Anthem

Jana-gana-mana adhinayak, jaya hey,
Bharat-bhagya vidhata.
Punjab-Sindh-Gujarat -Maratha-
Dravida-Utkala-Banga,
Vindhya-Himachal-Yamuna-Ganga,
Uchchala-jaladhi taranga,
Tava shubh name jage,
Tava shubh ashish maage,
Gahe tava jaya-gatha
Jana-gana-mangaldayak jaya hey,
Bharat-bhagya vidhata,
Jaya hey, jaya hey, jaya hey,
Jaya jaya jaya jaya hey.

-Rabindranath Tagore

National song

Vande Mataram!

Sujalam, Suphalam, Malayaja shitalam,

Shasyashyamalam, Mataram!

Vande Mataram!

Shubhrajyotsana, pulakitayaminim

Phullakusumita drumadala shobhinim,

Suhasinim sumadhura bhashinim,

Sukhadam varadam, Mataram!

Vande Mataram!

-Bankim Chandra Chattopadhyay

CALENDAR AND TIME

Months

- JANUARY
- FEBRUARY
- MARCH
- APRIL
- MAY
- JUNE
- JULY
- AUGUST
- SEPTEMBER
- OCTOBER
- NOVEMBER
- DECEMBER

Time

- 60 seconds = 1 minute
- 60 minutes = 1 hour
- 24 hours = 1 day
- 7 days = 1 week
- 4 weeks = 1 month
- 12 months = 1 year
- 365 days = 1 year
- 1 year = 52 weeks

Days of the Week

Sunday		6	13	20	27
Monday		7	14	21	28
Tuesday	1	8	15	22	29
Wednesday	2	9	16	23	30
Thursday	3	10	17	24	31
Friday	4	11	18	25	
Saturday	5	12	19	26	

OUR GREAT LEADERS

Mahatma Gandhi

Jawahar Lal Nehru

Bhagat Singh

Subhash Chandra Bose

Sardar Patel

Bal Gangadhar Tilak

Lal Bahadur Shastri

Bhimrao Ambedkar

Rajendra Prasad

Madan Mohan Malviya

Lala Lajpat Rai

Vinoba Bhave

Rajguru

Chandra Shekhar Azad

Indira Gandhi

Sarojini Naidu

ALL IN ONE

OUR CURRENCY

₹ 5 Note

₹10 Note

₹ 20 Note

₹ 50 Note

₹100 Note

₹ 500 Note

₹ 2000 Note

1 Rupee Coin   2 Rupee Coin   5 Rupee Coin   10 Rupee Coin

ALL IN ONE

90

tricolor

TYPES OF HOUSES

Bungalow

Castle

Apartment

Palace

Chawl

Cottage

Hut

Tree House

Wood House

Stone House

Tent

House Boat

Igloo

Cave

Hotel

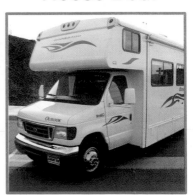
Caravan

ALL IN ONE

INDOOR GAMES

Table Tennis

Billiards

Boxing

Carrom

Chess

Gymnastics

Judo

Wrestling

Tug-of-War

Hide and Seek

Musical Chair

Scrabble

Playing Cards

Bowling

Play Station

Ludo

Blindman's Bluff

Puzzle

tricolor

Volleyball

Rowing

Badminton

Swing

Golf

Hockey

Kabaddi

Frog Race

Football

Cycling

Lawn Tennis

Equestrian

Duck Duck Goose

Kho- Kho

Cricket

Mountain Climbing

Basket ball

Baseball

tricolor

ALL IN ONE

MUSICAL INSTRUMENTS

Violin

Mandolin

Rattle

Sarod

Shehnai

Mridangam

Dholak

Guitar

Ghunghroo

Cymbals

Tambourine

Santoor

Veena

Drum

Mouth Organ

Flute

Bagpipe

Piano

Xylophone

Tabla

Iktara

Casio

Accordion

Bongo Drum

Harmonium

ALL IN ONE

Tricolor

MEANS OF COMMUNICATION

Fax Machine

Radio

Television

Telephone

Internet

Laptop

Cell-Phone

Walkie-Talkie

E-mail

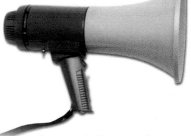
Loud Speaker

Pen Drive

Post Card

Newspaper

Dish Antenna

DVD

Magazine

Teleprinter

tricolor

ALL IN ONE

FURNITURE

Wardrobe

Cabinet

Sofa

Desk

Bean Bag

Bunk Bed

Foot Stool

Rocking Chair

Night Stand

Bench

Hammock

Pouffe

Table

Arm Chair

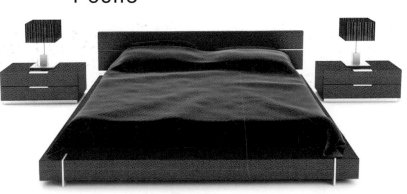

Bed

Lawn Chair

FLAGS

India

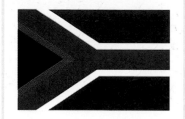

South Africa

Bangladesh

China

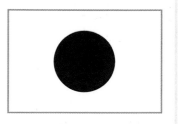

Japan

Nepal

Pakistan

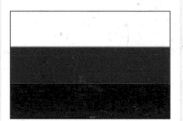

Russia

Singapore

Srilanka

Germany

United Kingdom

Canada

U.S.A.

Australia

New Zealand

tricolor

ALL IN ONE

DANCES OF INDIA

Sattaria
(Assam)

Odissi
(Odisha)

Mohiniattam
(Kerala)

Kuchipudi
(Andhra Pradesh)

Dandiya
(Gujarat)

Manipuri
(Manipur)

Kathakali
(Kerala)

Kathak
(North India)

Bharatnatyam
(Tamilnadu)

ELECTRICAL APPLIANCES

Microwave

Toaster

Tube Light

Air Cooler

Water Cooler

Iron

Lawn Mower

Air Conditioner

Mosquito Repellent

Juicer

Refrigerator

Ceiling Fan

Mixer

Dish Washer

Heat Convector

Geyser

Bulb

Washing Machine

ALL IN ONE

tricolor

KITCHEN ARTICLES

Gas Stove

Jug

Glass

Tea Set

Sieve

Spoon

Rolling Board & Pin

Ladle

Spatula

Pressure Cooker

Griddle

Cutting Board

Bowl

Dining Plate

Fork Set

Apron

Oven Mitt

Casserole

Mug

Frying Pan

ALL IN ONE

tricolor

WEATHERS

Cloudy

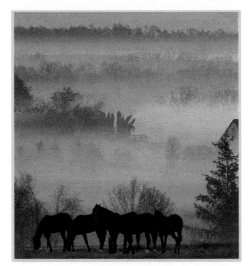

Foggy

Sunny

Rainy

Humid

Windy

Snowy

Dust Storm

Hail Storm

ALL IN ONE

tricolor books

ENVIRONMENTS

City

Forest

Desert

Grassland

Polar

Ocean

NATURAL DISASTERS

Hurricane

Typhoon

Flood

Earthquake

Landslide

Tornado

Tsunami

Cyclone

Avalanche

Volcano

Icestorm

Draught

tricolor

103

ALL IN ONE

| Airport | Cinema Hall | Railway Station | Bus Terminus |

| Police Station | Stadium | Park | School | Bank |

| Fire Station | Post Office | Beach | Hospital | Library |

MY FAMILY

Father

Mother

Aunt

Baby

Uncle

Rohan (Cousin)

Grandfather

Grandmother

Kanak (Me)

Mona (Sister)

Buster (Doggy)

Ronak (Brother)

ALL IN ONE

tricolor

BEDROOM

Fan

Wall Light

Curtains

Cupboard

Lamp

Pillow

Alarm Clock

Bed Sheet

Blanket

Mattress

Pyjamas

Cradle

Bed

Footmat

Floaters

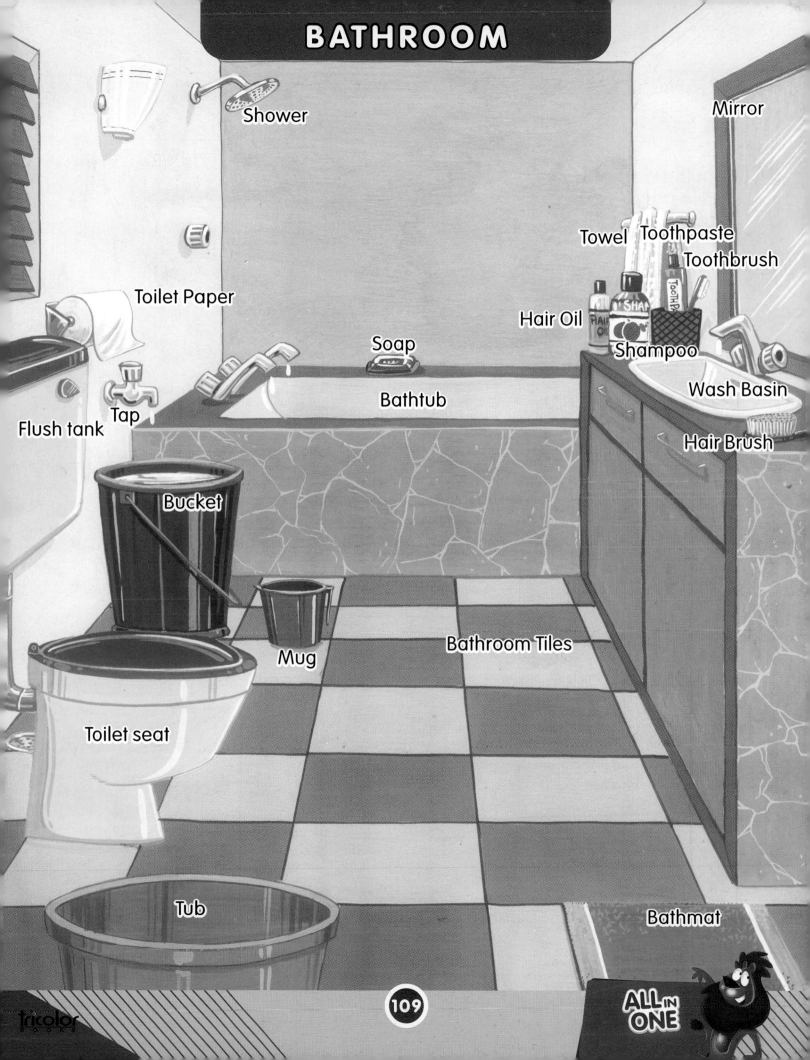

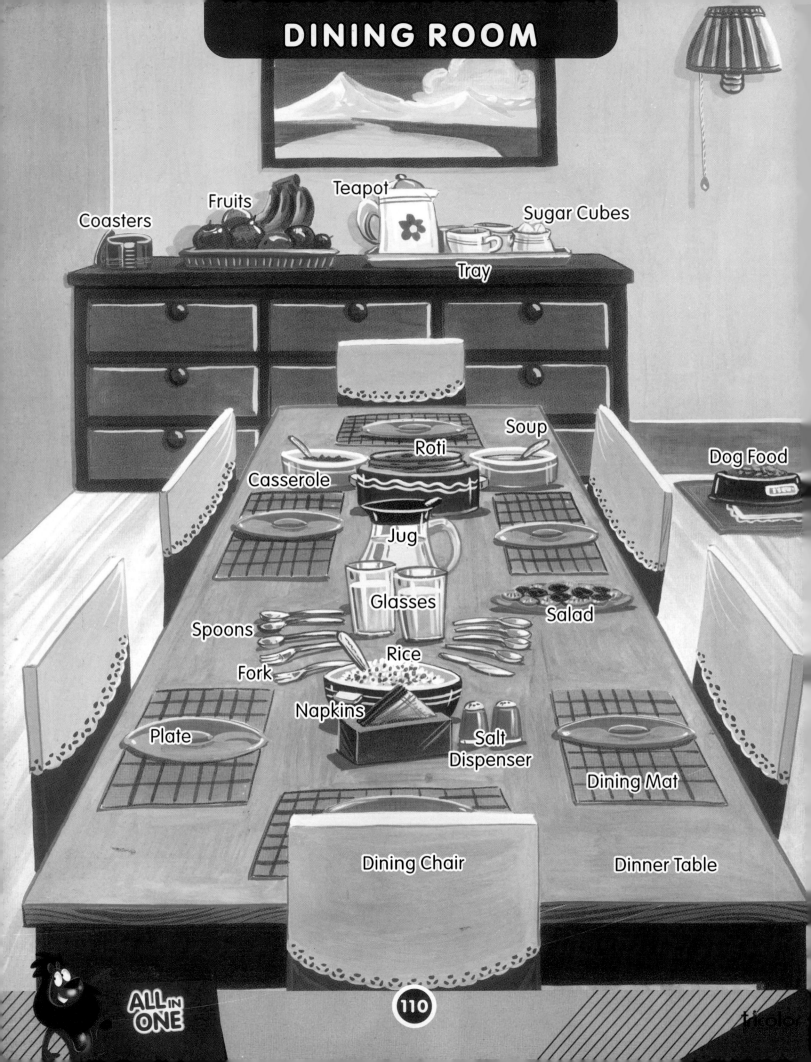

DINING ROOM

Coasters

Fruits

Teapot

Sugar Cubes

Tray

Dog Food

Soup

Roti

Casserole

Jug

Glasses

Salad

Spoons

Rice

Fork

Napkins

Plate

Salt Dispenser

Dining Mat

Dining Chair

Dinner Table

ALL IN ONE

tricolor

ALL IN ONE

DRAWING ROOM

Air Conditioner

Window

Wall Clock

Curtain

T.V.

Show Case

T.V. Cabinet

Showpiece

Cushions

Sofa Set

Vase

Centre Table

Carpet

Magazine

Remote

Telephone

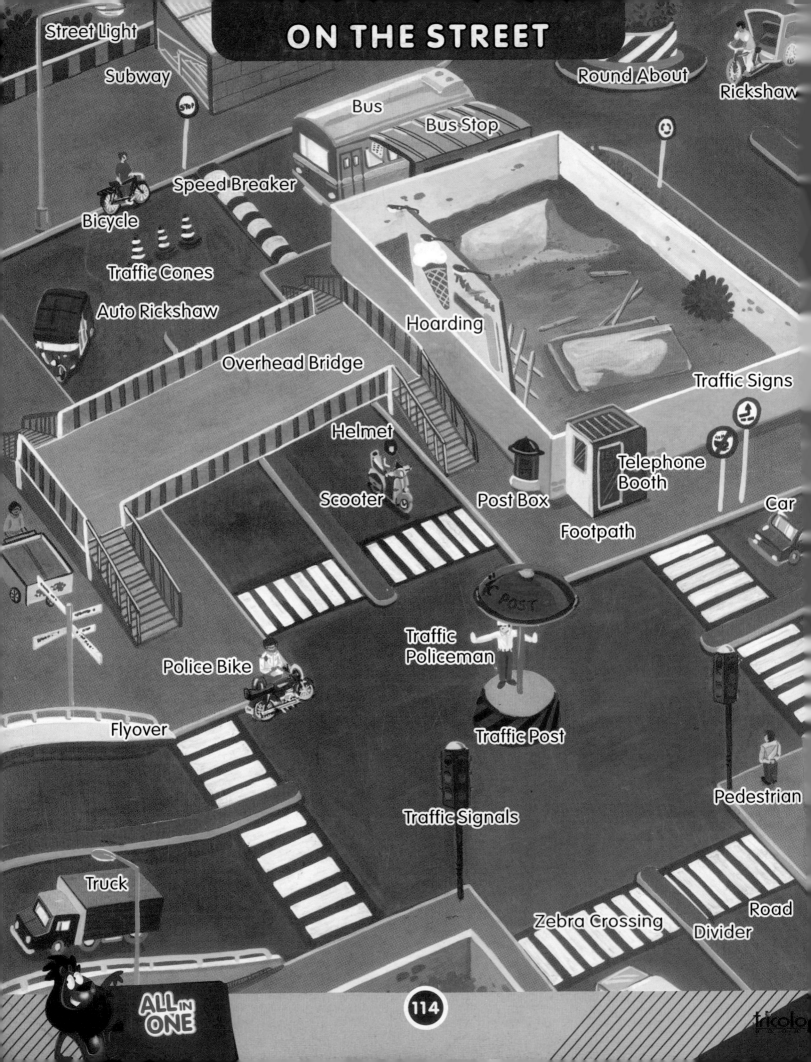

ON THE STREET

Street Light
Subway
Round About
Rickshaw
Bus
Bus Stop
Speed Breaker
Bicycle
Traffic Cones
Auto Rickshaw
Hoarding
Overhead Bridge
Traffic Signs
Helmet
Telephone Booth
Scooter
Post Box
Car
Footpath
Police Bike
Traffic Policeman
Flyover
Traffic Post
Pedestrian
Traffic Signals
Truck
Zebra Crossing
Road Divider

ALL IN ONE

tricolo

SHOPPING MALL

Signboard

Coffee Shop

Escalator

Lift

Salesman

Ice-cream

Customer

Shopping Cart

Cashier

Bar Code Reader

Can of Juice

Bag of Wheat

Milk Carton

Pack of Chips

Billing Counter

ALL IN ONE

VEGETABLE MARKET

Vegetable Seller

Stall

Broccoli

Labourer

Tempo

Cabbage

Tomato

Ginger

ORANGE

Fruits

PAPAYA

Lettuce

Weighing Scale

Beans

Capsicum

Weights

Lady Finger

Buyer

Carrot

Bottle Gourd

Potato

tricolor

ZOO

Giraffe

Elephant

Monkey

Grass

Tiger

Enclosure

Tree

Deer

Lion

Visitor

Zoo Attendant

Hippopotamus

Crocodile

Rabbits

Tortoise

ALL IN ONE

118

CIRCUS

Tent

Trapeze

Plate Spinning

Audience

Elephant Show

Unicyclist

Whip

Horse Show

Human Cannonball

Trampoline

Ring Master

Hoopers

Juggler

Magician

Clown

Fire Breathing

Tricolor

PARK

Tree

Birds

Fountain

Vines and Creepers

Bridge

Boundary Wall

Bench

Dragonfly

Pond

Frog

Duck and Ducklings

Jogging Track

Butterfly

Grass

Topiary

Water Pipe

Mud

Flowers

Gardener

Honeybee

Spider

Hedges

Spider Web

Gardening Tools

Caterpillar

Snail

ALL IN ONE

tricolor

One Two Buckle My Shoe

One, two, buckle my shoe;
Three, four, knock at the door;
Five, six, pick up sticks;
Seven, eight, lay them straight;
Nine, ten, a big fat hen.

Humpty Dumpty

Humpty Dumpty sat on a wall,
Humpty Dumpty had a great fall.
All the King's horses
And all the King's men
Couldn't put Humpty together again.

ALL IN ONE

Ring a ring o roses

Ring-a-ring o' roses,
A pocket full of posies,
A-tishoo, a-tishoo!
We all fall down.

Twinkle, Twinkle, Little Star

Twinkle, twinkle, little star,
How I wonder what you are!
Up above the world so high,
Like a diamond in the sky!

Johny Johny Yes Papa

Johnny, Johnny,
Yes, Papa.
Eating sugar?
No, Papa.
Telling lies?
No, Papa.
Open your mouth,
Ha! Ha! Ha!

Baa Baa Black Sheep

Baa, baa, black sheep,
Have you any wool?
Yes sir, yes sir,
Three bags full.

One for the master,
One for the dame.
And one for the little boy,
Who lives down the lane.

THE BUNDLE OF STICKS

An old man called his four sons. He asked each to bring two sticks. He told his boys to break one of the sticks they were holding. All the boys easily broke the stick. Then he took the remaining stick from all his sons and made a bundle of four sticks. He then told them to break the bundle of sticks. All the sons tried but were unable to break it. The father said,
"Unity brings strength. Stay together and no one will be able to defeat you."

THE PRODIGAL TREES

A Woodcutter once came to the jungle and requested the Trees to give him some wood. The Trees were kind hearted and so they gave the man some wood to provide his needs. The Man went back and used all the wood to make axes. He then went to the market and sold all the axes to other Woodcutters.

One day, the Woodcutters came to the jungle and cut the same trees whose wood was used to make the axes.

It's foolish to give anyone the means to destroy yourself!

tricolor

ALL in ONE

THE BAT, THE BIRDS AND THE BEASTS

Once a war was waging between the Beasts and the Birds, and both were building their own armies. But a Bat was so scared that he did not want to join any of the army.

So when the birds asked him to join them, he said that he was a beast. And when the beasts asked him, he said that he was a bird. The war began and ended soon. The Bat now wanted to join the celebrations.

So the Bat first went to the birds, but they turned against him. He then went to the beasts, but they kicked him out too.

One who helps no one, has no friends!